A Little Night Poetry

Megan Williamson

BookLeaf Publishing

Presentation by *BookLeaf Publishing*

Web: www.bookleafpub.com

E-mail: info@bookleafpub.com

ISBN : 9789357699754

First edition 2022

DEDICATION

For my beautiful family and in loving memory of my Nan, Mary.

ACKNOWLEDGEMENT

Thank you to my family for encouraging me to achieve a long time dream and thank you to Book Leaf Publishing for this opportunity.

Star Sailor

I'm a star sailor
I jump from star to star
I bath in there light
And admire them from afar

Stardust scatters the earth
Which i'll take in hand
The closest i'll get to holding one
A star's dust like sand

I'm a star sailor
With which i'll share the night
For star's are my greatest loves
And tonight my feast shall be on starlight

The Beach

You see lot's of pairs
Upon the golden shore
They come in all shapes and sizes
And many combinations

As the sun blazed down
Upon the smooth sand
Behind two pairs of deck chairs
Was a pair who caught my eye

An older lady with white hair
Looking down upon
A girl in a bright pink hat
Both bare foot in the sand

They both walk between the chairs
The girl chatting away
Whilst the woman listened well
As they strolled towards the water

The lady was devoted to the girl
She smiled at her
All her pride pouring out
And both absorbed in this happy place

A moment held in time

For the woman and the girl
A special memory for both
And will be all that's left one day

The girl will grow up
And many memories will fade
But never her special day
On the beach with Nan

Weathered Emotions

The clouds that shade my mind
Are far too real today
There scattered across the sky ahead
With no parting for a sun ray
Sometimes it feels like the clouds
Will never go away
And my mind like the clouds
Will always fog my day
But one thing about clouds
That I must try retain
One day the passing of the clouds
Will make way for the sun again

The rain turns the day
Into one sad and cold
The only feelings I can say
I often seem to hold
The trouble with rain
Is that it always seems to seep
Like my mind when in pain
The sadness seems to creep
But the beauty of the rain is
The thought of journey's end
To a home of warmth and comfort
The place where I will mend

The storm rages on
Like the battle inside me
As the elements march on
The anger consumes me
With each clash of thunder
The hate spills out everywhere
To some it's a sight of wonder
As I storm about without a care
But as the storm starts to calm
And the shame and regret set in
That power begins to lose it's charm
And the healing can now begin

The sun is joyous and bright
Like a weight has been removed
And as the sun ex-spells it's light
My mood continues to improve
With each step a spring
My mind for once settled
It feels like the world could sing
And life is no longer unsettled
As the sun begins to set
And the day draws to an end
There is no regret
And my mind feels like an old friend

The snow so crisp and pure
The freshest a mind can be
White covers the floor

And my soul is finally free
As the snow submerges all
It feels as all is clean
And all those doubts that cause my fall
Are gone from where they had been
Life is constantly changing
As is the world around us
And instead of rearranging
Take it all as it comes without fuss

Trinity of the World

H ope is what the world guides you to
O nce you have it you can do anything
P eace is the gift hope brings
E veryone has it, but some need help finding it

J oy is a moment the world gives to you
O ne that you treasure so dearly
Y earning for it until you realise you already
have it

L ove is what the world keeps from you
O ne small act of love goes far
V arities of love covers the planet
E veryone is always better for it

Work

This job is really boring
I'm almost snoring
Work all day
Earn our pay
Come back in the morning

Always running round
Worked into the ground
Always wrong
No work song
Not allowed to make a sound

Customers are always moaning
And the staff always groaning
How do we thrive
When all this is to stay alive
Life never been so boring

Can't keep the pace
I just hate this fucking place
Working is so boring
The boss is always roaring
I'm going to scream in their face

All they do is lie
They make the staff cry

And oh so boring
Life goes by soaring
And we'll work until we die

Jester

He is a funny man
He makes us laugh
Feel so high
Stop the sad tears
From the eye

Oh what a funny man
He is jolly as a clown
And as happy as Larry
The funniest guy around
He is the happiest happy

Such a funny man
He'll fall over again
Crack a couple of jokes
Do a juggle in the rain
The funniest things again and again

What a funny man
The jester's gesture is one that is sweet
That makes you smile with joy
The greatest man that you'll ever meet
He is the most jolly man

With the jester don't fear
Any strife of life

When the jester is near
The world will be bright
And everything will be alright

The Seven

Love is like a garden
Luscious, fresh and alive
But attention and care
Maintains it's welfare
For it to bloom and thrive

A dream is like a cloud
Delicate, pure and clear
But lost will it be
If efforts are empty
In the pursuit of a dream held dear

Memory is like a night sky
Sitting quietly all around
Like a star
Hidden afar
But can always be found

The soul is like a piece of clay
Upon a potter's wheel
A gentle hand
Can mark the land
The essence of the soul we seal

Death is like a door
Firmly ajar and secure

Then life's mortal blows
Slides the door to a close
And life is no more

Life is like a fair ground
Filled with souls and faces
It brings joy and laughter
And memories here after
And moments that time traces

Time is like nothing before
It's something you can't really measure
Death brings meaning
And Life brings great feeling
But Time is an endless treasure

Amelia

Fair thee well Amelia
When you take flight
The sky glows red
Filled with the buzz of Bessie
Your going away
Leaving the world behind
Across the ocean blue
But the world will cry
And our hearts will brake
For when you don't return
The world will be less bright
Lost in the sky
Dear Amelia
Where do you go
In which rocks do you hide
The sea conceals you from me
Don't you see
How much you've changed
The world around you
As you have changed me
Amelia,
You are gone
But I can't forget
How wonderful you are to me
So I hope you rest well
And your soul is free

I Love My Bed

I love my bed
It's my favourite place to be
A mound of pillows to lay my head
While snuggled in my bed

I love my bed
It's the best place in the world
For when i'm lead in my bed
My troubles have all fled

I love my bed
If you hadn't guessed
For any bad day or sharp words said
Melt away while in my bed

I love my bed
I'm in my bed right now
And in my bed
I shall remain
Until I am stone cold dead

The Farmer's Way

Last to bed
First to wake
Up again for another day
Your suit goes on
Boots tied tight
Sip your coffee on your way
When on the farm
You stretch and yawn
Start up the tractor and go spray
As the sun begins to rise
You wipe the dust from your eyes
The sun brings a good day
Your chugging along
With a farmer's song
Wouldn't have it any other way
Working away till the end
Light of the day gone for now
You pack up for another day
Heading home to folks you love
Settle your head for the night
That's the farmers way

Void

In my head
Full of dread
Thoughts are spinning round
Shadows creeping
The world still sleeping
My fears tightly bound
Sinking down
And I will drown
Feet can't touch the ground
Demons play
Angel astray
Hope no longer found
I've fallen into the void
I'm living in the void
My mind in shutdown
...
And I can't get out

Nursery Days

I once was a nursery nurse
I joined them one day
I needed to fill my purse
But there I would stay
For eight years, no more or less
And joined the mad ride
The world of chaotic mess
And I saw childcare from a different side

Some days I would cook
Many days filled with cuddles
Read a thousand times the same book
Or get sopping wet jumping in puddles
Hold the children when their sick
Clean up the explosive nappy round
Teach them what they can and can't lick
And nap time is sit silently, I don't make a sound

In Autumn we while away an afternoon outside
In Winter we warm up with a dance or two
In Spring we go on woodland walks and look for bugs that hide
And in Summer we splash in water trays, standing two by two
No two days are the same
Some days I had my lows

And sometimes it felt like a game
But those children always kept me on my toes

Children were my passion, I'd do anything to make them smile
And I noticed after a while, they helped me too
As they filled my head with questions and distractions for a while
They'd lift me up time again and I hope I did too
Sometimes they were a right pain
And I wonder what am I doing
But if I could do it all again
I wouldn't change a thing

Because there was love, care and joy
Within all that madness
And each child I loved, both girl and boy
And those days are the ones I will always miss

Mirror

Oh mirror on my wall
Why do I fear you most of all
For the person looking back
Isn't me at all

I can hide my face like a clown
Makeup, cream and gown
But the person looking back
Is one with a frown

I fill my head with comforting lies
And try to look through different eyes
But the person looking back
Pours with silent cries

For the woman stood before me
Is not the one I want to see
For the woman looking back
Is the only me I can be

I Still Exist

I still exist
But i'm not sure I want to
What's the point in living
If i'm not alive

If I don't exist
Pain will be removed
And I will no longer be wondering
Aimlessly through the dark

Why do I exist
I can't figure this out
There is no point or purpose
Life is meaningless

But if I don't exist
How will my mother feel
What will happen to my cat
How much sadness would I cause

I don't want to exist
And yet here I am
The world feels dark and cold
And emptiness fills my soul

But while I exist

I can comfort myself
With family, friends and people
Or a nice cup of tea

So I still exist
And I'm lost right now
But it won't last forever
Whereas death will

Pumpkin Patch

Come on down to my pumpkin patch
Where the pumpkins lay strewn
Come pick any one you want
I've grown them all for you
We have orange, white and green
Big, medium and small
And if none take your fancy
We have squashes too
So come on down to my pumpkin patch
There are many so take your pick
Help yourself to any you want
I have grown them all for you

Lucy

Oh Lucy
Can't you see
How beautiful you are to me
You see yourself in such a different way
From how I see you every single day
To me you are beauty and grace
With sparkling eyes and stunning face

Oh Lucy
Why do you look so sad
You are the best sister to be had
You tell yourself you have no brain
But your smartness is not one to contain
You think your weak with no strength of your own
But you are the bravest person that I have ever known

Oh Lucy
I wish you could see
The way you are to me
Your soul is pure and free
And you are as beautiful as beautiful can be
So please believe me when I say
You are the most wonderful woman I see everyday

Day Dreamer

I day dream away
Another day
Can't face the world again

The life in my head
Is better lead
Then the life I have

I can be
A better me
Not what the world sees

I deal with everything
Better then anything
I've dealt with before

Live a great life
None of the strife
Not a boring reality

A big dreamer
Constant streamer
The life I want

The place for me
Where I want to be

Please don't wake me up

I Know

I know your gone
I know the truth
I know that you've passed on
I know you are not here
I know your house is gone
I know I can't touch you anymore

But...

I feel like your with me
I feel your warmth inside
I feel you all around
I feel you in my heart
I feel you guiding me
I feel your hand in mine

And...
I know that your gone
But...
I feel you never left

Treasure

I have my very own treasure
But it does not shine
Nor does it glisten in the night
Or in the shape of a dime
My treasure is one you cannot find
Not hidden in a treasure chest
Nor buried in the sand
No booty below the sea
My treasure is not of gold
Nor a piece of eight
Or a jewel of any kind
My treasure is not of value
To those who are blind
For my very own treasure
Is not an object of any kind
My treasure is small
With ten tiny fingers
And the bluest blue eyes
And beautiful flowing hair
My treasure is not found
But made with love and care
My treasure can hold my hand
She's the apple of my eye
For my treasure is my god daughter
And she's worth so much more

Cup of Tea

Do you want a cup of tea?
Is the best question to ever be
One cup a day
Keeps the woes away
All from one cup of tea

Each warming sip comforts all
Especially after life's fall
And each golden cup
Fills us up
Till we again stand tall

Tea warms us in the rain
And tea soothes our pain
It hugs us when sad
A medicine when we feel bad
With tea life is less of a strain

Goodnight

Goodnight
Sleep tight
Watch the stars,
They shine so bright
And tonight
Everything,
Will be alright
For tonight
I'll be here
So sleep on through the night
The moon as your light
And i'll watch over you
So goodnight
Snuggle tight
I'll always be with you
Both day and night

www.ingramcontent.com/pod-product-compliance
Lightning Source LLC
Chambersburg PA
CBHW051749130826
49812CB00033B/1073
* 9 7 8 9 3 5 7 6 9 9 7 5 4 *